D1575280

Better Than Before

A DAY-BY-DAY JOURNAL

Copyright © 2015 by Gretchen Rubin

All rights reserved.
Published in the United States by Potter Style,
an imprint of the Crown Publishing Group,
a division of Penguin Random House LLC, New York.
www.crownpublishing.com
www.potterstyle.com

Potter Style is a trademark and POTTER STYLE
with colophon is a registered trademark of Penguin
Random House LLC.

Library of Congress cataloging-in-publication data
is available upon request.

ISBN 978-0-553-45929-6

Printed in China

Book design by Danielle Deschenes
Cover design based on the book design by Ben Wiseman

10 9 8 7 6 5 4 3 2 1

First Edition

Better Than Before

A DAY-BY-DAY JOURNAL

Change Your Habits,
Change Your Life

Gretchen Rubin

POTTER STYLE
NEW YORK

INTRODUCTION

Habits are the invisible architecture of daily life. We repeat about 40 percent of our behavior almost daily, so our habits shape our existence and our future. If we change our habits, we change our lives.

But that observation just raises the question: Okay, then, how do we change our habits? The fact is, no one-size-fits-all solution exists. It's easy to dream that if we copy the habits of productive, creative people, we'll win similar success. But we each must cultivate the habits that work for us—habits that are shaped to suit our individual temperament, interests, and values.

Some people do better when they start small; others, when they start big. Some people need to be held accountable; some defy accountability. Some thrive when they give themselves an occasional break from their good habits; others, when they never break the chain. No wonder habit formation is so hard.

This journal is a place to start thinking about and working on your habits—or thinking about how to help someone else change a habit.

It poses a series of questions to help you think about how to improve your habits. You'll be given an issue to consider and some space to write your response.

In these lines, you can monitor your progress and record the successes and stumbles you encounter along the way. Use each space as a daily diary—or a weekly check-in. The fifty-two prompts allow you to visit one prompt each week of the year, or to write and explore at your own pace.

Since we all approach habits differently, spend some time with the material in the opening pages of this journal. There, you'll find the twenty-one strategies of habit formation, as well as a Habits Manifesto.

This journal is meant to help you gain greater understanding of yourself, and by doing so, help you shape your habits to achieve the greatest success. Over time, it will provoke insights, spur conversation, and lead you toward a clearer vision of what you want to improve and how to do so.

The
TWENTY-ONE STRATEGIES
of HABIT FORMATION

You may think, "Twenty-one strategies! That's overwhelming." It might seem like a lot, but it's actually helpful, because you can choose the ones that work for you.

We're all different, so different strategies work for different people.

In fact, that's why the first two strategies relate to self-knowledge . . .

SELF-KNOWLEDGE

1. **The Four Tendencies:** To change your habits, you have to know yourself, and in particular, your Tendency—that is, whether you're an Upholder, Questioner, Obliger, or Rebel.

   When we try to form a new habit, we set an expectation for ourselves. We face *outer expectations* (like meeting a work deadline) and *inner expectations* (like keeping a New Year's resolution). Your Tendency describes how you respond to those expectations.

UPHOLDERS respond readily to both outer and inner expectations. They work hard to meet others' expectations—and their expectations for themselves.

QUESTIONERS question all expectations, and will meet an expectation only if they believe it's justified by reason, logic, and fairness; they follow only inner expectations.

OBLIGERS respond readily to outer expectations but struggle to meet inner expectations. They're motivated by *external accountability.*

REBELS resist all expectations, outer and inner alike. They choose to act from a sense of choice, of freedom. They resist control—even self-control.

2. **Distinctions:** Knowing yourself is so important that it's not enough to know your Tendency, you must also recognize your Distinctions. For instance . . .

   Are You a Marathoner or a Sprinter?
   Marathoners tend to work at a slow and steady clip and dislike the pressure of a deadline. Sprinters work in quick bursts and often deliberately wait for a deadline to spur them on.

   Lark or Owl?
   Research shows that morning people, or "Larks," really do differ from night people, or "Owls." If you're trying to start a habit of exercising more, and you're an Owl, scheduling a

5 a.m. gym time won't work for you; in fact, 8 a.m. probably won't work for you.

Finisher or Opener?

Some people love finishing, and some people love opening—both literally and figuratively. Finishers love the feeling of bringing a project to completion, and they're determined to use the last drop in the shampoo bottle; Openers thrill to the excitement of launching a new project and find pleasure in opening a fresh tube of toothpaste.

Novelty-Lover or Familiarity-Lover?

For familiarity-lovers, a habit becomes easier as it becomes familiar. Novelty-lovers may embrace habits more readily when they seem less . . . habit-like.

PILLARS OF HABITS

3. **Monitoring:** You manage what you monitor, so find a way to monitor whatever matters.

4. **Foundation:** First things first, and habits in these four areas help lay the foundation for further habit change. Begin your habit changes by making sure to:

   - get enough sleep
   - eat and drink right
   - move
   - unclutter

5. **Scheduling:** If it's on the calendar, it happens.

6. **Accountability:** You do better when you know someone's watching—even if *you're* the one doing the watching.

THE BEST TIME TO BEGIN

7. **First Steps:** It's enough to begin; if you're ready, begin now.

8. **Clean Slate:** Temporary becomes permanent, so start the way you want to continue.

9. **Lightning Bolt:** A single idea can change the habits of a lifetime overnight. Enormously powerful but hard to invoke on command.

DESIRE, EASE, AND EXCUSES

10. **Abstaining:** For some of us, moderation is too tough; it's easier to give up something altogether. (This strategy works very well for some people, and not at all for others.)

11. **Convenience:** Make it easy to do right and hard to go wrong.

12. **Inconvenience:** Change your surroundings, not yourself.

13. **Safeguards:** Plan to fail.

14. **Loophole-Spotting:** Don't kid yourself, don't give yourself excuses.

15. **Distraction:** Wait fifteen minutes.

16. **Reward:** The reward for a good habit is *the good habit,* and that's the reward to give yourself.

17. **Treats:** It's easier to ask more from yourself when you're giving more to yourself, so give yourself plenty of healthy treats.

18. **Pairing:** Only do X when you're doing Y. Simple but surprisingly effective.

UNIQUE, JUST LIKE EVERYONE ELSE

19. **Clarity:** The clearer you are about what you want, and how you expect yourself to behave, the more likely you are to stick to your habits.

20. **Identity:** Your habits reflect your identity, so if you struggle to change a particular habit, examine your identity.

21. **Other People:** Your habits rub off on other people, and their habits rub off on you. Plan accordingly.

THE HABITS MANIFESTO

1. What we do *every day* matters more than what we do *once in a while*.

2. Make it easy to do right and hard to go wrong.

3. Focus on actions, not outcomes.

4. By giving something up, we may gain.

5. Things often get harder before they get easier.

6. When we give more to ourselves, we can ask more from ourselves.

7. We're not very different from other people, but those differences are *very* important.

8. It's easier to change our surroundings than ourselves.

9. We can't make people change, but when we change, others may change.

10. We should make sure the things we do to feel *better* don't make us feel *worse*.

11. We manage what we monitor.

12. Once we're ready to begin, begin *now*.

Thinking about your habits can seem overwhelming. To help you identify what habits you might want to change, consider this list of the "Essential Seven":

THE ESSENTIAL SEVEN

1. Eat and drink more healthfully (give up sugar, eat more vegetables, drink less alcohol).

2. Exercise regularly.

3. Save, spend, and earn wisely (save regularly, pay down debt, donate to worthy causes, stick to a budget).

4. Rest, relax, and enjoy (stop watching TV in bed, turn off a cell phone, spend time in nature, cultivate silence, get enough sleep, spend less time in the car).

5. Accomplish more, stop procrastinating (practice an instrument, work without interruption, learn a language, maintain a blog).

6. Simplify, clear, clean, and organize (make the bed, file regularly, put keys away in the same place, recycle).

7. Engage more deeply in relationships—with other people, with God, with the world (call friends, volunteer, have more sex, spend more time with family, attend religious services).

The same habit can satisfy different needs. A morning walk in the park might be a form of exercise (#2); a way to rest and enjoy (#4); or, in the company of a friend, a way to engage more deeply in a relationship (#7). And people value different habits.

Keep the Chain Going

Before you begin writing in this journal, identify a few habits that you'd like to adopt, or changes you'd like to make. The writing prompts on the following pages are designed to help you harness the power of habits to make change in your own life.

After you've spent some time answering the question for the week, you'll find a space to record and catalog your habit-formation goals and progress in the weekly habits tracker like the one on the following page.

Along with the space for reflection, this simple tool will help illuminate your own challenges and successes, day by day, toward a better you. Whenever you read this, and wherever you are, you're in the right place to begin.

HABITS TRACKER ✴ List the habits you're working on this week.

1. Brought lunch to work from home
2. Meditated
3.
4.

Each day, mark off the box when you successfully implement the habit.

HABIT 1	HABIT 2	HABIT 3	HABIT 4
MON ☒	MON ☒	MON ☐	MON ☐
TUE ☒	TUE ☒	TUE ☐	TUE ☐
WED ☐	WED ☐	WED ☐	WED ☐
THU ☒	THU ☒	THU ☐	THU ☐
FRI ☐	FRI ☒	FRI ☐	FRI ☐
SAT ☐	SAT ☐	SAT ☐	SAT ☐
SUN ☐	SUN ☐	SUN ☐	SUN ☐

There's a magic to the beginning of anything. All those old sayings are really true: Don't get it perfect, get it going. A journey of a thousand miles begins with a single step. Nothing is more exhausting than the task that's never started, and strangely, starting is often far harder than continuing.

Spend some time pondering a habit or behavior you have been dreading starting—and take a first step, no matter how small.

_____

_____

_____

_____

_____

_____

_____

_____

_____

_____

_____

_____

HABITS TRACKER ✳ List the habits you're working on this week.

1. _____

2. _____

3. _____

4. _____

Each day, mark off the box when you successfully implement the habit.

HABIT 1	HABIT 2	HABIT 3	HABIT 4
MON ☐	MON ☐	MON ☐	MON ☐
TUE ☐	TUE ☐	TUE ☐	TUE ☐
WED ☐	WED ☐	WED ☐	WED ☐
THU ☐	THU ☐	THU ☐	THU ☐
FRI ☐	FRI ☐	FRI ☐	FRI ☐
SAT ☐	SAT ☐	SAT ☐	SAT ☐
SUN ☐	SUN ☐	SUN ☐	SUN ☐

Beware of *finish lines* when working to change habits: "I ran the marathon." "I did a 30-day sugar detox." There are many behaviors that we want to follow indefinitely—to run, to write, to eat healthfully—but a finish line divides behavior into "start" and "stop," and all too often, the "stop" becomes permanent.

What steps can you take to avoid the notion of a finish line? Have you given thought to how your habit will continue after you pass a finish line?

_____

_____

_____

_____

_____

_____

_____

_____

_____

_____

_____

*

HABITS TRACKER ✳ List the habits you're working on this week.

1. _____

2. _____

3. _____

4. _____

Each day, mark off the box when you successfully implement the habit.

HABIT 1	HABIT 2	HABIT 3	HABIT 4
MON ☐	MON ☐	MON ☐	MON ☐
TUE ☐	TUE ☐	TUE ☐	TUE ☐
WED ☐	WED ☐	WED ☐	WED ☐
THU ☐	THU ☐	THU ☐	THU ☐
FRI ☐	FRI ☐	FRI ☐	FRI ☐
SAT ☐	SAT ☐	SAT ☐	SAT ☐
SUN ☐	SUN ☐	SUN ☐	SUN ☐

"There is a myth, sometimes widespread, that a person need do only inner work . . . that a man is entirely responsible for his own problems; and that to cure himself, he need only change himself. . . . The fact is, a person is so formed by his surroundings, that his state of harmony depends entirely on his harmony with his surroundings."

—Christopher Alexander, _The Timeless Way of Building_

How are your habits shaped by your environment? What can you do this week to change your surroundings to improve your habits?

*

HABITS TRACKER * List the habits you're working on this week.

1. _____

2. _____

3. _____

4. _____

Each day, mark off the box when you successfully implement the habit.

HABIT 1	HABIT 2	HABIT 3	HABIT 4
MON ☐	MON ☐	MON ☐	MON ☐
TUE ☐	TUE ☐	TUE ☐	TUE ☐
WED ☐	WED ☐	WED ☐	WED ☐
THU ☐	THU ☐	THU ☐	THU ☐
FRI ☐	FRI ☐	FRI ☐	FRI ☐
SAT ☐	SAT ☐	SAT ☐	SAT ☐
SUN ☐	SUN ☐	SUN ☐	SUN ☐

Sometimes the easiest way to set up a habit is simply to hide it in your daily life. Want to save for a college fund? Instead of worrying each month about how much to put aside, set up a savings account that deducts the money automatically—you've created the habit of saving without having to think about it.

It's a Secret of Adulthood: Make it easy to do right and hard to go wrong.

What's a "hidden habit" that you can adopt to make your life better?

_____

_____

_____

_____

_____

_____

_____

_____

_____

_____

_____

_____

_____

HABITS TRACKER ✳ List the habits you're working on this week.

1. _____

2. _____

3. _____

4. _____

Each day, mark off the box when you successfully implement the habit.

HABIT 1	HABIT 2	HABIT 3	HABIT 4
MON ☐	MON ☐	MON ☐	MON ☐
TUE ☐	TUE ☐	TUE ☐	TUE ☐
WED ☐	WED ☐	WED ☐	WED ☐
THU ☐	THU ☐	THU ☐	THU ☐
FRI ☐	FRI ☐	FRI ☐	FRI ☐
SAT ☐	SAT ☐	SAT ☐	SAT ☐
SUN ☐	SUN ☐	SUN ☐	SUN ☐

A milestone event—a marriage, a diagnosis, a death, an anniversary, hitting bottom, a birthday, an accident, a midlife crisis, a long journey taken alone—often triggers a "Lightning Bolt," when we're smacked with some new idea that jolts us into change.

Have you ever experienced a "Lightning Bolt" in your life that helped you change your habit overnight?

_____

_____

_____

_____

_____

_____

_____

_____

_____

_____

_____

_____

_____

✳

HABITS TRACKER ✳ List the habits you're working on this week.

1. _____

2. _____

3. _____

4. _____

Each day, mark off the box when you successfully implement the habit.

HABIT 1	HABIT 2	HABIT 3	HABIT 4
MON ☐	MON ☐	MON ☐	MON ☐
TUE ☐	TUE ☐	TUE ☐	TUE ☐
WED ☐	WED ☐	WED ☐	WED ☐
THU ☐	THU ☐	THU ☐	THU ☐
FRI ☐	FRI ☐	FRI ☐	FRI ☐
SAT ☐	SAT ☐	SAT ☐	SAT ☐
SUN ☐	SUN ☐	SUN ☐	SUN ☐

We should pay special attention to any habit that we try to *hide*. The desire to prevent family, friends, or coworkers from acting as witnesses—from seeing what's on the computer screen or knowing how much time or money we're spending on a habit—is a clue that, in some way, our actions don't reflect our values.

What habit do you—consciously or unconsciously—hide from others?

_____

_____

_____

_____

_____

_____

_____

_____

_____

_____

_____

_____

_____

HABITS TRACKER ✳ List the habits you're working on this week.

1. _____

2. _____

3. _____

4. _____

Each day, mark off the box when you successfully implement the habit.

HABIT 1	HABIT 2	HABIT 3	HABIT 4
MON ☐	MON ☐	MON ☐	MON ☐
TUE ☐	TUE ☐	TUE ☐	TUE ☐
WED ☐	WED ☐	WED ☐	WED ☐
THU ☐	THU ☐	THU ☐	THU ☐
FRI ☐	FRI ☐	FRI ☐	FRI ☐
SAT ☐	SAT ☐	SAT ☐	SAT ☐
SUN ☐	SUN ☐	SUN ☐	SUN ☐

Persisting with a habit can be particularly hard when the habit doesn't yield flashy results.

While it's satisfying to know that you're doing something that's good for you, you may not achieve instant accolades or glorious outcomes from your habits. If, however, you accept that habit change can be dull and even tiresome, after a while, the habit truly takes over and proves itself by making your life better than before.

Getting through this tiresome period of habit formation is tough. Recall instances in your past when you succeeded in getting through the early stages of habit formation. What helped you to persist?

_____

_____

_____

_____

_____

_____

_____

_____

_____

*

HABITS TRACKER ✳ List the habits you're working on this week.

1. _____

2. _____

3. _____

4. _____

Each day, mark off the box when you successfully implement the habit.

HABIT 1	HABIT 2	HABIT 3	HABIT 4
MON ☐	MON ☐	MON ☐	MON ☐
TUE ☐	TUE ☐	TUE ☐	TUE ☐
WED ☐	WED ☐	WED ☐	WED ☐
THU ☐	THU ☐	THU ☐	THU ☐
FRI ☐	FRI ☐	FRI ☐	FRI ☐
SAT ☐	SAT ☐	SAT ☐	SAT ☐
SUN ☐	SUN ☐	SUN ☐	SUN ☐

For people who want to eat and drink more healthfully, keeping a food journal can be extremely effective. For instance, one study showed that dieters who kept a food journal six or seven days a week lost twice as much weight as people who did so once a week or not at all.

Try keeping a food journal for just a single week. What do you think you'll discover about your eating habits? Look back after the week's end to see how your assumptions compare to reality.

_____

_____

_____

_____

_____

_____

_____

_____

_____

_____

_____

1. _____

2. _____

3. _____

4. _____

Each day, mark off the box when you successfully implement the habit.

HABIT 1	HABIT 2	HABIT 3	HABIT 4
MON ☐	MON ☐	MON ☐	MON ☐
TUE ☐	TUE ☐	TUE ☐	TUE ☐
WED ☐	WED ☐	WED ☐	WED ☐
THU ☐	THU ☐	THU ☐	THU ☐
FRI ☐	FRI ☐	FRI ☐	FRI ☐
SAT ☐	SAT ☐	SAT ☐	SAT ☐
SUN ☐	SUN ☐	SUN ☐	SUN ☐

Even good habits have drawbacks as well as benefits. Habits speed time, because when every day is the same, experience shortens and blurs. That's why the first *month* at a new job seems to last longer than the fifth year at that job. And, as it speeds time, habit also deadens. Habit makes it dangerously easy to become numb to our own existence.

What pleasant habit has become such a part of your daily architecture that you don't notice it anymore? Write about one habit, and how you might savor it more deeply.

_____

_____

_____

_____

_____

_____

_____

_____

_____

_____

_____

_____

*

HABITS TRACKER * List the habits you're working on this week.

1. _____

2. _____

3. _____

4. _____

Each day, mark off the box when you successfully implement the habit.

HABIT 1	HABIT 2	HABIT 3	HABIT 4
MON ☐	MON ☐	MON ☐	MON ☐
TUE ☐	TUE ☐	TUE ☐	TUE ☐
WED ☐	WED ☐	WED ☐	WED ☐
THU ☐	THU ☐	THU ☐	THU ☐
FRI ☐	FRI ☐	FRI ☐	FRI ☐
SAT ☐	SAT ☐	SAT ☐	SAT ☐
SUN ☐	SUN ☐	SUN ☐	SUN ☐

"In the acquisition of a new habit, or the leaving off of an old one, we must take care to launch ourselves with as strong and decided an initiative as possible. . . . Never suffer an exception to occur till the new habit is securely rooted in your life. Each lapse is like the letting fall of a ball of string which one is carefully winding up; a single slip undoes more than a great many turns will wind again."

—William James, *Psychology: The Briefer Course*

What are your biggest habit "slips"?

_____

_____

_____

_____

_____

_____

_____

_____

_____

_____

_____

*

HABITS TRACKER ✳ List the habits you're working on this week.

1. _____

2. _____

3. _____

4. _____

Each day, mark off the box when you successfully implement the habit.

HABIT 1	HABIT 2	HABIT 3	HABIT 4
MON ☐	MON ☐	MON ☐	MON ☐
TUE ☐	TUE ☐	TUE ☐	TUE ☐
WED ☐	WED ☐	WED ☐	WED ☐
THU ☐	THU ☐	THU ☐	THU ☐
FRI ☐	FRI ☐	FRI ☐	FRI ☐
SAT ☐	SAT ☐	SAT ☐	SAT ☐
SUN ☐	SUN ☐	SUN ☐	SUN ☐

Research suggests that when we have conflicting goals, we don't manage ourselves well. We become anxious and paralyzed, and we may end up doing nothing.

Is there an area where your values conflict? For instance, are you caught between family responsibilities and work responsibilities? Between goofing off and having an orderly, pleasant home? If you're having trouble with a specific habit, consider whether it raises a conflict in your values.

_____

_____

_____

_____

_____

_____

_____

_____

_____

_____

_____

✳

HABITS TRACKER * List the habits you're working on this week.

1. _____

2. _____

3. _____

4. _____

Each day, mark off the box when you successfully implement the habit.

HABIT 1	HABIT 2	HABIT 3	HABIT 4
MON ☐	MON ☐	MON ☐	MON ☐
TUE ☐	TUE ☐	TUE ☐	TUE ☐
WED ☐	WED ☐	WED ☐	WED ☐
THU ☐	THU ☐	THU ☐	THU ☐
FRI ☐	FRI ☐	FRI ☐	FRI ☐
SAT ☐	SAT ☐	SAT ☐	SAT ☐
SUN ☐	SUN ☐	SUN ☐	SUN ☐

Of all the strategies of habit change, the Strategy of Treats is the most fun. Unlike a reward, which must be earned or justified, a "treat" is a small pleasure or indulgence that we give to ourselves *just because we want it*. We don't have to be "good" to get it, we don't earn it or justify it. "Treats" may sound like a self-indulgent, frivolous strategy, but it's not. Because forming good habits can be draining, treats can play an important role. It's a Secret of Adulthood: If you give more to yourself, you can ask more from yourself. Self-regard isn't selfish.

What simple, healthy treats can you add to your life "just because"? Spend the week identifying new treats to give yourself that will help you feel energized and cared for.

_____

_____

_____

_____

_____

_____

_____

_____

_____

✳

HABITS TRACKER ✳ List the habits you're working on this week.

1. _____

2. _____

3. _____

4. _____

Each day, mark off the box when you successfully implement the habit.

HABIT 1	HABIT 2	HABIT 3	HABIT 4
MON ☐	MON ☐	MON ☐	MON ☐
TUE ☐	TUE ☐	TUE ☐	TUE ☐
WED ☐	WED ☐	WED ☐	WED ☐
THU ☐	THU ☐	THU ☐	THU ☐
FRI ☐	FRI ☐	FRI ☐	FRI ☐
SAT ☐	SAT ☐	SAT ☐	SAT ☐
SUN ☐	SUN ☐	SUN ☐	SUN ☐

When we stumble with a habit, it's important not to judge ourselves harshly. Although some people assume that strong feelings of guilt or shame act as safeguards to help people stick to good habits, the opposite is true. People who feel less guilt and who show compassion toward themselves in the face of failure are better able to regain self-control, while people who feel deeply guilty and full of self-blame struggle more.

Be kind to yourself. A stumble may prevent a fall, so try to learn from a stumble. Write about how you can accept your habit "stumbles" and move forward without guilt or shame.

_____

_____

_____

_____

_____

_____

_____

_____

_____

_____

_____

*

HABITS TRACKER ✳ List the habits you're working on this week.

1. _____

2. _____

3. _____

4. _____

Each day, mark off the box when you successfully implement the habit.

HABIT 1	HABIT 2	HABIT 3	HABIT 4
MON ☐	MON ☐	MON ☐	MON ☐
TUE ☐	TUE ☐	TUE ☐	TUE ☐
WED ☐	WED ☐	WED ☐	WED ☐
THU ☐	THU ☐	THU ☐	THU ☐
FRI ☐	FRI ☐	FRI ☐	FRI ☐
SAT ☐	SAT ☐	SAT ☐	SAT ☐
SUN ☐	SUN ☐	SUN ☐	SUN ☐

_____ / / to / / _____

A key for understanding many bad habits? Impulsivity. Impulsive people have trouble delaying satisfaction and considering long-term consequences; they find it difficult to plan ahead; once they start a task, they struggle to stick with it. The Strategy of Inconvenience helps us resist acting impulsively, because the harder it is to do something, the harder it is to do it impulsively.

Record some ways to make your bad habits harder to do on impulse. For instance, to stop hitting the snooze button, move the alarm clock across the room. To watch less TV, keep the remote control on a high shelf.

_____

_____

_____

_____

_____

_____

_____

_____

_____

_____

HABITS TRACKER ✳ List the habits you're working on this week.

1. _____

2. _____

3. _____

4. _____

Each day, mark off the box when you successfully implement the habit.

HABIT 1	HABIT 2	HABIT 3	HABIT 4
MON ☐	MON ☐	MON ☐	MON ☐
TUE ☐	TUE ☐	TUE ☐	TUE ☐
WED ☐	WED ☐	WED ☐	WED ☐
THU ☐	THU ☐	THU ☐	THU ☐
FRI ☐	FRI ☐	FRI ☐	FRI ☐
SAT ☐	SAT ☐	SAT ☐	SAT ☐
SUN ☐	SUN ☐	SUN ☐	SUN ☐

Be on the watch for the "This Doesn't Count" Loophole: We tell ourselves that for some reason, this circumstance doesn't count. "I'm on vacation." "It's the holiday season." "I'm sick." "This is a onetime thing."

Can you think of times when you excused a bad habit by saying, "This doesn't count"?

_____

_____

_____

_____

_____

_____

_____

_____

_____

_____

_____

_____

_____

_____

HABITS TRACKER ✳ List the habits you're working on this week.

1. _____

2. _____

3. _____

4. _____

Each day, mark off the box when you successfully implement the habit.

HABIT 1	HABIT 2	HABIT 3	HABIT 4
MON ☐	MON ☐	MON ☐	MON ☐
TUE ☐	TUE ☐	TUE ☐	TUE ☐
WED ☐	WED ☐	WED ☐	WED ☐
THU ☐	THU ☐	THU ☐	THU ☐
FRI ☐	FRI ☐	FRI ☐	FRI ☐
SAT ☐	SAT ☐	SAT ☐	SAT ☐
SUN ☐	SUN ☐	SUN ☐	SUN ☐

Habits make change possible by freeing us from decision making and from using self-control. "Am I going to brush my teeth when I wake up?" "Am I going to take this pill?" Don't worry about continually making healthy choices; make one healthy choice and then stop choosing.

Record some ways you can "stop choosing" on the road to healthier habits.

_____

_____

_____

_____

_____

_____

_____

_____

_____

_____

_____

_____

_____

*

HABITS TRACKER ✳ List the habits you're working on this week.

1. _____

2. _____

3. _____

4. _____

Each day, mark off the box when you successfully implement the habit.

HABIT 1	HABIT 2	HABIT 3	HABIT 4
MON ☐	MON ☐	MON ☐	MON ☐
TUE ☐	TUE ☐	TUE ☐	TUE ☐
WED ☐	WED ☐	WED ☐	WED ☐
THU ☐	THU ☐	THU ☐	THU ☐
FRI ☐	FRI ☐	FRI ☐	FRI ☐
SAT ☐	SAT ☐	SAT ☐	SAT ☐
SUN ☐	SUN ☐	SUN ☐	SUN ☐

Many people succeed best when they keep their starting steps as small and manageable as possible; by doing so, they gain the habit of the habit and the feeling of mastery. They begin their new yoga routine by doing three poses, or start work on a big writing project by drafting a single sentence in a writing session.

List some small steps for the week that you can take to gain mastery of your habit.

_____

_____

_____

_____

_____

_____

_____

_____

_____

_____

_____

_____

HABITS TRACKER * List the habits you're working on this week.

1. _____

2. _____

3. _____

4. _____

Each day, mark off the box when you successfully implement the habit.

HABIT 1	HABIT 2	HABIT 3	HABIT 4
MON ☐	MON ☐	MON ☐	MON ☐
TUE ☐	TUE ☐	TUE ☐	TUE ☐
WED ☐	WED ☐	WED ☐	WED ☐
THU ☐	THU ☐	THU ☐	THU ☐
FRI ☐	FRI ☐	FRI ☐	FRI ☐
SAT ☐	SAT ☐	SAT ☐	SAT ☐
SUN ☐	SUN ☐	SUN ☐	SUN ☐

If starting small isn't helpful, start big.

For some people, surprisingly, it's easier to make a major change than a minor change. If a habit changes very gradually, they may lose interest, give way under stress, or dismiss the change as insignificant.

Do you find it easier to start big? If so, set yourself a challenging habit to work toward.

_____

_____

_____

_____

_____

_____

_____

_____

_____

_____

_____

_____

*

HABITS TRACKER ＊ List the habits you're working on this week.

1. _____

2. _____

3. _____

4. _____

Each day, mark off the box when you successfully implement the habit.

HABIT 1	HABIT 2	HABIT 3	HABIT 4
MON ☐	MON ☐	MON ☐	MON ☐
TUE ☐	TUE ☐	TUE ☐	TUE ☐
WED ☐	WED ☐	WED ☐	WED ☐
THU ☐	THU ☐	THU ☐	THU ☐
FRI ☐	FRI ☐	FRI ☐	FRI ☐
SAT ☐	SAT ☐	SAT ☐	SAT ☐
SUN ☐	SUN ☐	SUN ☐	SUN ☐

Habits grow strongest and fastest when they're repeated in predictable ways, and for most of us, putting an activity on the schedule tends to lock us into doing it.

Put it on the calendar! Spend a week adding the habits you want to acquire into your calendar. Use your smart phone's calendar, email reminders, a notebook calendar, whatever it takes to keep you on track.

*

HABITS TRACKER ✳ List the habits you're working on this week.

1. _____

2. _____

3. _____

4. _____

Each day, mark off the box when you successfully implement the habit.

HABIT 1	HABIT 2	HABIT 3	HABIT 4
MON ☐	MON ☐	MON ☐	MON ☐
TUE ☐	TUE ☐	TUE ☐	TUE ☐
WED ☐	WED ☐	WED ☐	WED ☐
THU ☐	THU ☐	THU ☐	THU ☐
FRI ☐	FRI ☐	FRI ☐	FRI ☐
SAT ☐	SAT ☐	SAT ☐	SAT ☐
SUN ☐	SUN ☐	SUN ☐	SUN ☐

Counterintuitively, minor temptations to our habits can be more challenging than major temptations. A student might not say, "I'm going to spend the afternoon at the beach with my friends," but he'll think, "I'll check out sports highlights for fifteen minutes before I start working," then fifteen more, then fifteen more, and pretty soon three hours have gone by.

Little temptations sometimes slip past our guard. Where do you let small temptations grow into major habit lapses?

_____

_____

_____

_____

_____

_____

_____

_____

_____

_____

_____

_____

_____

*

HABITS TRACKER * List the habits you're working on this week.

1. _____

2. _____

3. _____

4. _____

Each day, mark off the box when you successfully implement the habit.

HABIT 1	HABIT 2	HABIT 3	HABIT 4
MON ☐	MON ☐	MON ☐	MON ☐
TUE ☐	TUE ☐	TUE ☐	TUE ☐
WED ☐	WED ☐	WED ☐	WED ☐
THU ☐	THU ☐	THU ☐	THU ☐
FRI ☐	FRI ☐	FRI ☐	FRI ☐
SAT ☐	SAT ☐	SAT ☐	SAT ☐
SUN ☐	SUN ☐	SUN ☐	SUN ☐

_____ / / to / / _____

"All our life, so far as it has definite form, is but a mass of habits—practical, emotional, and intellectual—systematically organized for our weal or woe, and bearing us irresistibly toward our destiny."

—William James, _Talks to Teachers and Students on Psychology_

Use the questions below to learn more about yourself, then consider your answers as you plan your habits:

_____

_____

_____

_____

_____

_____

_____

_____

_____

_____

_____

*

HABITS TRACKER * List the habits you're working on this week.

1. _____

2. _____

3. _____

4. _____

Each day, mark off the box when you successfully implement the habit.

HABIT 1	HABIT 2	HABIT 3	HABIT 4
MON ☐	MON ☐	MON ☐	MON ☐
TUE ☐	TUE ☐	TUE ☐	TUE ☐
WED ☐	WED ☐	WED ☐	WED ☐
THU ☐	THU ☐	THU ☐	THU ☐
FRI ☐	FRI ☐	FRI ☐	FRI ☐
SAT ☐	SAT ☐	SAT ☐	SAT ☐
SUN ☐	SUN ☐	SUN ☐	SUN ☐

People get a real lift when they put things in their place, clear surfaces, and get rid of things that don't work or aren't used. This surge of energy makes it easier to ask more of ourselves, to use our self-control, and to stick to a challenging habit.

For most people, outer order leads to inner calm. Where in your life is clutter getting out of control? This week make an effort to find one area in which to conquer clutter.

_____

*

HABITS TRACKER * List the habits you're working on this week.

1. _____

2. _____

3. _____

4. _____

Each day, mark off the box when you successfully implement the habit.

HABIT 1	HABIT 2	HABIT 3	HABIT 4
MON ☐	MON ☐	MON ☐	MON ☐
TUE ☐	TUE ☐	TUE ☐	TUE ☐
WED ☐	WED ☐	WED ☐	WED ☐
THU ☐	THU ☐	THU ☐	THU ☐
FRI ☐	FRI ☐	FRI ☐	FRI ☐
SAT ☐	SAT ☐	SAT ☐	SAT ☐
SUN ☐	SUN ☐	SUN ☐	SUN ☐

As Montaigne observed, "The infancies of all things are feeble and weak. We must keep our eyes open at their beginnings; you cannot find the danger then because it is so small: once it has grown, you cannot find the cure."

Develop a strategy of safeguards against your bad habits. Start by eliminating the cues that lead to temptation—whether it's changing your morning walk so you don't pass by the donut shop, or putting a temporary block on your favorite social media sites.

_____

_____

_____

_____

_____

_____

_____

_____

_____

_____

_____

*

HABITS TRACKER ✳ List the habits you're working on this week.

1. _____

2. _____

3. _____

4. _____

Each day, mark off the box when you successfully implement the habit.

HABIT 1	HABIT 2	HABIT 3	HABIT 4
MON ☐	MON ☐	MON ☐	MON ☐
TUE ☐	TUE ☐	TUE ☐	TUE ☐
WED ☐	WED ☐	WED ☐	WED ☐
THU ☐	THU ☐	THU ☐	THU ☐
FRI ☐	FRI ☐	FRI ☐	FRI ☐
SAT ☐	SAT ☐	SAT ☐	SAT ☐
SUN ☐	SUN ☐	SUN ☐	SUN ☐

Often, in the busyness of everyday life, we neglect to make time for the things that we enjoy most. We know that the habit of riding a bike, practicing the guitar, cooking, or reading would make us happier—but somehow, we never make time for those activities. But what if we had more time?

If you magically had an extra hour in the day to do whatever you liked, what would you do with it? Once you've answered that question, think of ways to change your habits so that you make time in your calendar for that missing element.

HABITS TRACKER * List the habits you're working on this week.

1. _____

2. _____

3. _____

4. _____

Each day, mark off the box when you successfully implement the habit.

HABIT 1	HABIT 2	HABIT 3	HABIT 4
MON ☐	MON ☐	MON ☐	MON ☐
TUE ☐	TUE ☐	TUE ☐	TUE ☐
WED ☐	WED ☐	WED ☐	WED ☐
THU ☐	THU ☐	THU ☐	THU ☐
FRI ☐	FRI ☐	FRI ☐	FRI ☐
SAT ☐	SAT ☐	SAT ☐	SAT ☐
SUN ☐	SUN ☐	SUN ☐	SUN ☐

Be on the watch for the "Lack of Control" Loophole. Weirdly, we often have an illusion of control over things we can't control—"If I spend a lot of time worrying, the plane is less likely to crash"; "If I play my lucky numbers, I'll win the lottery eventually"—but deny control over things we can control—"If my cell phone buzzes, I have to check it." We argue that circumstances force us to break a habit, but often we have more control than we admit.

Where in your life do you act as though you lack control? Look for areas where you make excuses like "These are irresistible," "I don't have any time to do that," etc. Do you have more control than you assume?

_____

_____

_____

_____

_____

_____

_____

_____

_____

*

HABITS TRACKER ✳ List the habits you're working on this week.

1. _____

2. _____

3. _____

4. _____

Each day, mark off the box when you successfully implement the habit.

HABIT 1	HABIT 2	HABIT 3	HABIT 4
MON ☐	MON ☐	MON ☐	MON ☐
TUE ☐	TUE ☐	TUE ☐	TUE ☐
WED ☐	WED ☐	WED ☐	WED ☐
THU ☐	THU ☐	THU ☐	THU ☐
FRI ☐	FRI ☐	FRI ☐	FRI ☐
SAT ☐	SAT ☐	SAT ☐	SAT ☐
SUN ☐	SUN ☐	SUN ☐	SUN ☐

"Abstainers" do better when they follow all-or-nothing habits. They're not tempted by things that they've decided are off-limits, but they can't have "just one bite." "Moderators," by contrast, find that an occasional indulgence both heightens their pleasure and strengthens their resolve; they get panicky or rebellious at the thought of "never" getting or doing something.

Are you an abstainer or a moderator? If you've tried abstaining or moderating without success when facing a certain strong temptation—with french fries or with TV, for instance—try the other strategy.

_____

_____

_____

_____

_____

_____

_____

_____

_____

_____

HABITS TRACKER ✳ List the habits you're working on this week.

1. _____

2. _____

3. _____

4. _____

Each day, mark off the box when you successfully implement the habit.

HABIT 1	HABIT 2	HABIT 3	HABIT 4
MON ☐	MON ☐	MON ☐	MON ☐
TUE ☐	TUE ☐	TUE ☐	TUE ☐
WED ☐	WED ☐	WED ☐	WED ☐
THU ☐	THU ☐	THU ☐	THU ☐
FRI ☐	FRI ☐	FRI ☐	FRI ☐
SAT ☐	SAT ☐	SAT ☐	SAT ☐
SUN ☐	SUN ☐	SUN ☐	SUN ☐

One way to lock ourselves into a habit is to use a "commitment device"—that is, some mechanism that bolsters our habits by locking us into a decision. We can't change our minds, or if we do, we're heavily penalized. The lowly china piggy bank is a child's commitment device, and adults may open a Christmas account, which levies charges against account holders who withdraw savings before the holiday.

What commitment devices can you add to your habit choices?

_____

_____

_____

_____

_____

_____

_____

_____

_____

_____

_____

_____

*

HABITS TRACKER ✳ List the habits you're working on this week.

1. _____

2. _____

3. _____

4. _____

Each day, mark off the box when you successfully implement the habit.

HABIT 1	HABIT 2	HABIT 3	HABIT 4
MON ☐	MON ☐	MON ☐	MON ☐
TUE ☐	TUE ☐	TUE ☐	TUE ☐
WED ☐	WED ☐	WED ☐	WED ☐
THU ☐	THU ☐	THU ☐	THU ☐
FRI ☐	FRI ☐	FRI ☐	FRI ☐
SAT ☐	SAT ☐	SAT ☐	SAT ☐
SUN ☐	SUN ☐	SUN ☐	SUN ☐

Sometimes we adopt a habit to signal the identity we want others to see, or we may adopt a habit to signal an identity we *wish* we had—like the guy who keeps his desk messy because he thinks that the disorder makes him look more creative. We can also get locked into identities that aren't good for us: "a workaholic," "a perfectionist," "the life of the party," "the responsible one."

Spend some time thinking about how you might need to redefine your identity in order to change a habit.

_____

_____

_____

_____

_____

_____

_____

_____

_____

_____

_____

*

HABITS TRACKER * List the habits you're working on this week.

1. _____

2. _____

3. _____

4. _____

Each day, mark off the box when you successfully implement the habit.

HABIT 1	HABIT 2	HABIT 3	HABIT 4
MON ☐	MON ☐	MON ☐	MON ☐
TUE ☐	TUE ☐	TUE ☐	TUE ☐
WED ☐	WED ☐	WED ☐	WED ☐
THU ☐	THU ☐	THU ☐	THU ☐
FRI ☐	FRI ☐	FRI ☐	FRI ☐
SAT ☐	SAT ☐	SAT ☐	SAT ☐
SUN ☐	SUN ☐	SUN ☐	SUN ☐

The very words we choose to characterize our habits can make them seem more or less appealing. "Engagement time" sounds more interesting than "email time"; "playing the piano" sounds like more fun than "practicing the piano"; and what sounds more attractive, a "personal retreat day" or a "catch-up day," a "ditch day" or a "mandatory vacation day"?

Spend some time to reframe your habits. Can you find a way to recharacterize a habit and its effects on your life?

_____

_____

_____

_____

_____

_____

_____

_____

_____

_____

_____

_____

＊

HABITS TRACKER ✳ List the habits you're working on this week.

1. _____

2. _____

3. _____

4. _____

Each day, mark off the box when you successfully implement the habit.

HABIT 1	HABIT 2	HABIT 3	HABIT 4
MON ☐	MON ☐	MON ☐	MON ☐
TUE ☐	TUE ☐	TUE ☐	TUE ☐
WED ☐	WED ☐	WED ☐	WED ☐
THU ☐	THU ☐	THU ☐	THU ☐
FRI ☐	FRI ☐	FRI ☐	FRI ☐
SAT ☐	SAT ☐	SAT ☐	SAT ☐
SUN ☐	SUN ☐	SUN ☐	SUN ☐

Although people often assume that cravings intensify over time, research shows that with active distraction, urges—even strong urges—usually subside within about fifteen minutes.

Whether it's exercise, junk food, or something else, try using the "fifteen-minute rule" to distract yourself from breaking a good habit or giving in to a bad one.

_____

_____

_____

_____

_____

_____

_____

_____

_____

_____

_____

_____

*

HABITS TRACKER * List the habits you're working on this week.

1. _____

2. _____

3. _____

4. _____

Each day, mark off the box when you successfully implement the habit.

HABIT 1	HABIT 2	HABIT 3	HABIT 4
MON ☐	MON ☐	MON ☐	MON ☐
TUE ☐	TUE ☐	TUE ☐	TUE ☐
WED ☐	WED ☐	WED ☐	WED ☐
THU ☐	THU ☐	THU ☐	THU ☐
FRI ☐	FRI ☐	FRI ☐	FRI ☐
SAT ☐	SAT ☐	SAT ☐	SAT ☐
SUN ☐	SUN ☐	SUN ☐	SUN ☐

Beware of the "Fake Self-Actualization" Loophole. Invoking this loophole often looks like an embrace of life or an acceptance of self, so that the failure to pursue a habit seems life-affirming—almost spiritual. For most of us, however, the real aim isn't to enjoy a few pleasures right now, but to build habits that will make us happy over the long term. Sometimes, that means giving up something in the present, or demanding more from ourselves.

Be on the watch for Fake Self-Actualization Loopholes: "You only live once." "I'll be sorry if I don't at least try it." "I should celebrate this special occasion." "Life is too short not to live a little."

_____

_____

_____

_____

_____

_____

_____

_____

_____

_____

HABITS TRACKER ✳ List the habits you're working on this week.

1. _____

2. _____

3. _____

4. _____

Each day, mark off the box when you successfully implement the habit.

HABIT 1	HABIT 2	HABIT 3	HABIT 4
MON ☐	MON ☐	MON ☐	MON ☐
TUE ☐	TUE ☐	TUE ☐	TUE ☐
WED ☐	WED ☐	WED ☐	WED ☐
THU ☐	THU ☐	THU ☐	THU ☐
FRI ☐	FRI ☐	FRI ☐	FRI ☐
SAT ☐	SAT ☐	SAT ☐	SAT ☐
SUN ☐	SUN ☐	SUN ☐	SUN ☐

In the area of health alone, our habits can have a profound effect. Poor diet, inactivity, smoking, and drinking are among the leading causes of illness and death in the United States—and these are health habits within our control. In many ways, our habits are our destiny.

Whether it's smoking, not wearing a helmet while riding a bike, or ignoring important dietary concerns, do you have any habits that are actually dangerous to your health?

_____

_____

_____

_____

_____

_____

_____

_____

_____

_____

_____

✳

HABITS TRACKER ✳ List the habits you're working on this week.

1. _____

2. _____

3. _____

4. _____

Each day, mark off the box when you successfully implement the habit.

HABIT 1	HABIT 2	HABIT 3	HABIT 4
MON ☐	MON ☐	MON ☐	MON ☐
TUE ☐	TUE ☐	TUE ☐	TUE ☐
WED ☐	WED ☐	WED ☐	WED ☐
THU ☐	THU ☐	THU ☐	THU ☐
FRI ☐	FRI ☐	FRI ☐	FRI ☐
SAT ☐	SAT ☐	SAT ☐	SAT ☐
SUN ☐	SUN ☐	SUN ☐	SUN ☐

Watch out for the "what the heck" effect: "I broke my diet by eating this one mini-cupcake, so what the heck, now I'm going to eat the whole box."

Remember that a misstep is simply that—a stumble doesn't have to lead to a fall. One lapse doesn't have to mean complete relapse into a bad habit.

_____

_____

_____

_____

_____

_____

_____

_____

_____

_____

_____

_____

_____

_____

✳

HABITS TRACKER ✳ List the habits you're working on this week.

1. _____

2. _____

3. _____

4. _____

Each day, mark off the box when you successfully implement the habit.

HABIT 1	HABIT 2	HABIT 3	HABIT 4
MON ☐	MON ☐	MON ☐	MON ☐
TUE ☐	TUE ☐	TUE ☐	TUE ☐
WED ☐	WED ☐	WED ☐	WED ☐
THU ☐	THU ☐	THU ☐	THU ☐
FRI ☐	FRI ☐	FRI ☐	FRI ☐
SAT ☐	SAT ☐	SAT ☐	SAT ☐
SUN ☐	SUN ☐	SUN ☐	SUN ☐

_____ / / to / / _____

"When conviction is present, and temptation out of sight, we do not easily conceive how any reasonable being can deviate from his true interest."

—Samuel Johnson, *The Idler*, No. 27

Can you devise safeguards for your habits to protect them from common stumbling blocks? Try to anticipate and minimize temptation—both in your environment and in your own mind—and plan for failure.

*

HABITS TRACKER ✳ List the habits you're working on this week.

1. _____

2. _____

3. _____

4. _____

Each day, mark off the box when you successfully implement the habit.

HABIT 1	HABIT 2	HABIT 3	HABIT 4
MON ☐	MON ☐	MON ☐	MON ☐
TUE ☐	TUE ☐	TUE ☐	TUE ☐
WED ☐	WED ☐	WED ☐	WED ☐
THU ☐	THU ☐	THU ☐	THU ☐
FRI ☐	FRI ☐	FRI ☐	FRI ☐
SAT ☐	SAT ☐	SAT ☐	SAT ☐
SUN ☐	SUN ☐	SUN ☐	SUN ☐

Be alert for the "Moral Licensing" Loophole. In moral licensing, we give ourselves permission to do something "bad" (eat potato chips, bust the budget), because we've been "good." We reason that we've earned it or deserve it.

Do any of these statements sound familiar?

"I've been losing weight steadily on this diet, so it will be okay for me to cut a few corners."

"I've been so good about meditating, I deserve a day off."

"I've done so many holiday errands, I deserve to buy a little something for myself."

_____

_____

_____

_____

_____

_____

_____

_____

_____

_____

_____

*

HABITS TRACKER * List the habits you're working on this week.

1. _____

2. _____

3. _____

4. _____

Each day, mark off the box when you successfully implement the habit.

HABIT 1	HABIT 2	HABIT 3	HABIT 4
MON ☐	MON ☐	MON ☐	MON ☐
TUE ☐	TUE ☐	TUE ☐	TUE ☐
WED ☐	WED ☐	WED ☐	WED ☐
THU ☐	THU ☐	THU ☐	THU ☐
FRI ☐	FRI ☐	FRI ☐	FRI ☐
SAT ☐	SAT ☐	SAT ☐	SAT ☐
SUN ☐	SUN ☐	SUN ☐	SUN ☐

Many people report that they want to feel less stressed. But "stress" is a vague word, and because it doesn't pinpoint any concrete problems, it doesn't suggest solutions. When we confess to being stressed, we often blur the connection between the way we act and the way we feel.

What do you mean—specifically—when you say "I'm stressed"? For instance, if you're "stressed" at work, are you exhausted from lack of sleep? Do you have a difficult relationship with a boss or colleague? Do you find your work boring or meaningless? Do you have too many responsibilities? Are you too rushed? Do you have to attend too many meetings? Etc.

_____

_____

_____

_____

_____

_____

_____

_____

_____

*

HABITS TRACKER ✳ List the habits you're working on this week.

1. _____

2. _____

3. _____

4. _____

Each day, mark off the box when you successfully implement the habit.

HABIT 1	HABIT 2	HABIT 3	HABIT 4
MON ☐	MON ☐	MON ☐	MON ☐
TUE ☐	TUE ☐	TUE ☐	TUE ☐
WED ☐	WED ☐	WED ☐	WED ☐
THU ☐	THU ☐	THU ☐	THU ☐
FRI ☐	FRI ☐	FRI ☐	FRI ☐
SAT ☐	SAT ☐	SAT ☐	SAT ☐
SUN ☐	SUN ☐	SUN ☐	SUN ☐

One way to get a better understanding of yourself is to imagine yourself as a fabulous Hollywood celebrity—and you, like all fabulous celebrities, have a manager who watches out for you. When people make demands on you, your manager says things like, "He can't stay out that late, he needs his sleep," or "She can't do that right now, because she has a lot on her plate."

Be your own "manager." Imagine that you're the "manager" who's looking out for you—telling you and other people what's best for you.

_____

_____

_____

_____

_____

_____

_____

_____

_____

_____

_____

_____

_____

HABITS TRACKER ✳ List the habits you're working on this week.

1. _____

2. _____

3. _____

4. _____

Each day, mark off the box when you successfully implement the habit.

HABIT 1	HABIT 2	HABIT 3	HABIT 4
MON ☐	MON ☐	MON ☐	MON ☐
TUE ☐	TUE ☐	TUE ☐	TUE ☐
WED ☐	WED ☐	WED ☐	WED ☐
THU ☐	THU ☐	THU ☐	THU ☐
FRI ☐	FRI ☐	FRI ☐	FRI ☐
SAT ☐	SAT ☐	SAT ☐	SAT ☐
SUN ☐	SUN ☐	SUN ☐	SUN ☐

Often, when we try repeatedly to form a habit that we desire, we fail because we want to reap its benefits without paying the price it demands. Consider that stark line from John Gardner, so significant for habits, when he observed, "Every time you break the law you pay, and every time you obey the law you pay."

Keeping a good habit costs us: It may cost time, energy, and money, and it may mean forgoing pleasures and opportunities—but not keeping a good habit also has its cost. So which cost do you want to pay? What will make your life happier in the long run?

_____

_____

_____

_____

_____

_____

_____

_____

_____

_____

_____

_____

_____

*

HABITS TRACKER ✳ List the habits you're working on this week.

1. _____

2. _____

3. _____

4. _____

Each day, mark off the box when you successfully implement the habit.

HABIT 1	HABIT 2	HABIT 3	HABIT 4
MON ☐	MON ☐	MON ☐	MON ☐
TUE ☐	TUE ☐	TUE ☐	TUE ☐
WED ☐	WED ☐	WED ☐	WED ☐
THU ☐	THU ☐	THU ☐	THU ☐
FRI ☐	FRI ☐	FRI ☐	FRI ☐
SAT ☐	SAT ☐	SAT ☐	SAT ☐
SUN ☐	SUN ☐	SUN ☐	SUN ☐

Because certain habits most directly strengthen self-control, we do well to begin by tackling the Foundation habits that help us to:

1. sleep
2. move
3. eat and drink right
4. unclutter

Foundation habits tend to reinforce each other—for instance, exercise helps people sleep, and sleep helps people do everything better—so they're a good place to start for any kind of habit change. Are there habits you wish to adopt that can act as a foundation habit?

_____

_____

_____

_____

_____

_____

_____

_____

_____

_____

_____

HABITS TRACKER ✳ List the habits you're working on this week.

1. _____

2. _____

3. _____

4. _____

Each day, mark off the box when you successfully implement the habit.

HABIT 1	HABIT 2	HABIT 3	HABIT 4
MON ☐	MON ☐	MON ☐	MON ☐
TUE ☐	TUE ☐	TUE ☐	TUE ☐
WED ☐	WED ☐	WED ☐	WED ☐
THU ☐	THU ☐	THU ☐	THU ☐
FRI ☐	FRI ☐	FRI ☐	FRI ☐
SAT ☐	SAT ☐	SAT ☐	SAT ☐
SUN ☐	SUN ☐	SUN ☐	SUN ☐

/ /   to   / /

It's easy to assume that we act because of the way we feel, but to a great degree, we feel because of the way we act. For instance, if you act with more energy, you'll feel more energetic, and conversely, if you act apathetic, you'll feel more apathetic.

Try to "act the way I want to feel." Spend some time in the space below exploring the question of how, exactly, do you want to feel? In what areas do you wish to feel differently, and what small actions can you take to do so? What challenges will you face?

_____

_____

_____

_____

_____

_____

_____

_____

_____

_____

_____

_____

*

HABITS TRACKER * List the habits you're working on this week.

1. _____

2. _____

3. _____

4. _____

Each day, mark off the box when you successfully implement the habit.

HABIT 1	HABIT 2	HABIT 3	HABIT 4
MON ☐	MON ☐	MON ☐	MON ☐
TUE ☐	TUE ☐	TUE ☐	TUE ☐
WED ☐	WED ☐	WED ☐	WED ☐
THU ☐	THU ☐	THU ☐	THU ☐
FRI ☐	FRI ☐	FRI ☐	FRI ☐
SAT ☐	SAT ☐	SAT ☐	SAT ☐
SUN ☐	SUN ☐	SUN ☐	SUN ☐

When we're in a social situation, usually we want to fit in, and this desire to be in step with others can become a stumbling block for good habits. For instance, perhaps you feel compelled to have a drink or dessert when you're at dinner with work colleagues or with your family—even if you don't want it.

Write about your own personal challenges when it comes to habits and social situations.

_____

_____

_____

_____

_____

_____

_____

_____

_____

_____

_____

_____

*

HABITS TRACKER * List the habits you're working on this week.

1. _____

2. _____

3. _____

4. _____

Each day, mark off the box when you successfully implement the habit.

HABIT 1	HABIT 2	HABIT 3	HABIT 4
MON ☐	MON ☐	MON ☐	MON ☐
TUE ☐	TUE ☐	TUE ☐	TUE ☐
WED ☐	WED ☐	WED ☐	WED ☐
THU ☐	THU ☐	THU ☐	THU ☐
FRI ☐	FRI ☐	FRI ☐	FRI ☐
SAT ☐	SAT ☐	SAT ☐	SAT ☐
SUN ☐	SUN ☐	SUN ☐	SUN ☐

/ / to / /

Watch out for the "Concern for Others" Loophole. We tell ourselves that we're acting out of consideration for others and making generous, unselfish decisions. Or we decide we must do something in order to fit into a social situation.

Do you ever find yourself saying things like, "So many people need me, there's no time to focus on my own health," "It would be rude to go to a friend's birthday party and not eat a piece of cake," "I don't want to seem holier-than-thou"?

HABITS TRACKER ✳ List the habits you're working on this week.

1. _____

2. _____

3. _____

4. _____

Each day, mark off the box when you successfully implement the habit.

HABIT 1	HABIT 2	HABIT 3	HABIT 4
MON ☐	MON ☐	MON ☐	MON ☐
TUE ☐	TUE ☐	TUE ☐	TUE ☐
WED ☐	WED ☐	WED ☐	WED ☐
THU ☐	THU ☐	THU ☐	THU ☐
FRI ☐	FRI ☐	FRI ☐	FRI ☐
SAT ☐	SAT ☐	SAT ☐	SAT ☐
SUN ☐	SUN ☐	SUN ☐	SUN ☐

Physical activity is the magical elixir of practically everything. Exercise relieves anxiety, boosts energy and mood, improves memory, sharpens executive function, and contributes to weight maintenance. It both energizes us and calms us.

An exercise routine is a common goal for many people—but we often choose a program or a goal that's not a good fit for us. As you consider exercise options, think about: Do you enjoy spending time outdoors, or do you prefer not to deal with weather? Are you motivated by competition? Do you enjoy exercising to strong music and a driving beat, or do you prefer a quiet background? Do you respond well to some form of external accountability (a trainer, a running group), or is internal accountability sufficient? Do you like to challenge yourself with exercise (learning a new skill, pushing yourself physically), or do you prefer familiar activities? Do you like sports and games?

*

HABITS TRACKER ✴ List the habits you're working on this week.

1. _____

2. _____

3. _____

4. _____

Each day, mark off the box when you successfully implement the habit.

HABIT 1	HABIT 2	HABIT 3	HABIT 4
MON ☐	MON ☐	MON ☐	MON ☐
TUE ☐	TUE ☐	TUE ☐	TUE ☐
WED ☐	WED ☐	WED ☐	WED ☐
THU ☐	THU ☐	THU ☐	THU ☐
FRI ☐	FRI ☐	FRI ☐	FRI ☐
SAT ☐	SAT ☐	SAT ☐	SAT ☐
SUN ☐	SUN ☐	SUN ☐	SUN ☐

A highly effective habit-formation tool is to make detailed plans of action for keeping good habits. "If_____ happens, then I will do____."

Create your own "if-then" plans for your habits. This way, you anticipate habit challenges that may arise, so you don't make decisions in the heat of the moment—you've already decided how to behave.

_____

_____

_____

_____

_____

_____

_____

_____

_____

_____

_____

_____

_____

HABITS TRACKER ✳ List the habits you're working on this week.

1. _____

2. _____

3. _____

4. _____

Each day, mark off the box when you successfully implement the habit.

HABIT 1	HABIT 2	HABIT 3	HABIT 4
MON ☐	MON ☐	MON ☐	MON ☐
TUE ☐	TUE ☐	TUE ☐	TUE ☐
WED ☐	WED ☐	WED ☐	WED ☐
THU ☐	THU ☐	THU ☐	THU ☐
FRI ☐	FRI ☐	FRI ☐	FRI ☐
SAT ☐	SAT ☐	SAT ☐	SAT ☐
SUN ☐	SUN ☐	SUN ☐	SUN ☐

Sometimes a single unexpected question can illuminate a hidden aspect of your life. A question like "Do you tend to blame other people, or do you blame yourself?" can give you a fresh perspective and push you to think about aspects of your habits in new ways.

Scan the questions below and write about the ones that strike you as the most relevant to you and your everyday habits.

---

*

HABITS TRACKER ✳ List the habits you're working on this week.

1. _____

2. _____

3. _____

4. _____

Each day, mark off the box when you successfully implement the habit.

HABIT 1	HABIT 2	HABIT 3	HABIT 4
MON ☐	MON ☐	MON ☐	MON ☐
TUE ☐	TUE ☐	TUE ☐	TUE ☐
WED ☐	WED ☐	WED ☐	WED ☐
THU ☐	THU ☐	THU ☐	THU ☐
FRI ☐	FRI ☐	FRI ☐	FRI ☐
SAT ☐	SAT ☐	SAT ☐	SAT ☐
SUN ☐	SUN ☐	SUN ☐	SUN ☐

To a truly astonishing degree, our habits are shaped by sheer convenience. The amount of effort, time, or decision making required by an action has a huge influence on habit formation. We're far more likely to do something if it's convenient, and less likely if it's not.

In what ways can you make your good habits more convenient and your bad habits less convenient?

_____

_____

_____

_____

_____

_____

_____

_____

_____

_____

_____

*

HABITS TRACKER ✳ List the habits you're working on this week.

1. _____

2. _____

3. _____

4. _____

Each day, mark off the box when you successfully implement the habit.

HABIT 1	HABIT 2	HABIT 3	HABIT 4
MON ☐	MON ☐	MON ☐	MON ☐
TUE ☐	TUE ☐	TUE ☐	TUE ☐
WED ☐	WED ☐	WED ☐	WED ☐
THU ☐	THU ☐	THU ☐	THU ☐
FRI ☐	FRI ☐	FRI ☐	FRI ☐
SAT ☐	SAT ☐	SAT ☐	SAT ☐
SUN ☐	SUN ☐	SUN ☐	SUN ☐

"What difference does one bite make?" "I just want a taste, that's all." Hah! As La Rochefoucauld wrote, "It is much easier to extinguish a first desire than to satisfy all of those that follow it."

When it comes to your habits, what ways can you avoid the "just one bite" approach?

_____

_____

_____

_____

_____

_____

_____

_____

_____

_____

_____

_____

_____

*

HABITS TRACKER ✳ List the habits you're working on this week.

1. _____

2. _____

3. _____

4. _____

Each day, mark off the box when you successfully implement the habit.

HABIT 1	HABIT 2	HABIT 3	HABIT 4
MON ☐	MON ☐	MON ☐	MON ☐
TUE ☐	TUE ☐	TUE ☐	TUE ☐
WED ☐	WED ☐	WED ☐	WED ☐
THU ☐	THU ☐	THU ☐	THU ☐
FRI ☐	FRI ☐	FRI ☐	FRI ☐
SAT ☐	SAT ☐	SAT ☐	SAT ☐
SUN ☐	SUN ☐	SUN ☐	SUN ☐

When studying habits, certain familiar tensions appear: whether to accept yourself or expect more from yourself; whether to embrace the present or consider the future; whether to think about yourself or forget yourself. Because habit formation often requires us to relinquish something we want, a constant challenge is: How can you deprive yourself of something without feeling deprived?

When we feel deprived, we feel entitled to compensate ourselves—often in ways that undermine our good habits. Are there ways you can eliminate feeling deprived so that you're not tempted to indulge in a bad habit?

_____

_____

_____

_____

_____

_____

_____

_____

_____

_____

_____

✳

HABITS TRACKER ✳ List the habits you're working on this week.

1. _____

2. _____

3. _____

4. _____

Each day, mark off the box when you successfully implement the habit.

HABIT 1	HABIT 2	HABIT 3	HABIT 4
MON ☐	MON ☐	MON ☐	MON ☐
TUE ☐	TUE ☐	TUE ☐	TUE ☐
WED ☐	WED ☐	WED ☐	WED ☐
THU ☐	THU ☐	THU ☐	THU ☐
FRI ☐	FRI ☐	FRI ☐	FRI ☐
SAT ☐	SAT ☐	SAT ☐	SAT ☐
SUN ☐	SUN ☐	SUN ☐	SUN ☐

Whenever we monitor a behavior, we tend to do a much better job of managing it, and to monitor effectively, it's crucial to identify precisely what action is monitored. When we guess what we're doing, we're often wildly inaccurate—for instance, we tend to underestimate how much we eat and overestimate how much we exercise.

Find a way to monitor an important activity—a food diary, a daily expense log, an exercise tracker, a chart of family dinners. Do you find that monitoring that habit makes it easier to stick to it?

_____

_____

_____

_____

_____

_____

_____

_____

_____

_____

_____

*

HABITS TRACKER ✳ List the habits you're working on this week.

1. _____

2. _____

3. _____

4. _____

Each day, mark off the box when you successfully implement the habit.

HABIT 1	HABIT 2	HABIT 3	HABIT 4
MON ☐	MON ☐	MON ☐	MON ☐
TUE ☐	TUE ☐	TUE ☐	TUE ☐
WED ☐	WED ☐	WED ☐	WED ☐
THU ☐	THU ☐	THU ☐	THU ☐
FRI ☐	FRI ☐	FRI ☐	FRI ☐
SAT ☐	SAT ☐	SAT ☐	SAT ☐
SUN ☐	SUN ☐	SUN ☐	SUN ☐

Are you a "public resolver" or a "private resolver"? For some people, the public announcement of a habit or goal makes all the difference; some people do better when they keep their resolutions private.

Do you succeed better when you go public with a habit that you want to change, or when you keep it private?

_____

_____

_____

_____

_____

_____

_____

_____

_____

_____

_____

_____

_____

*

HABITS TRACKER * List the habits you're working on this week.

1. _____

2. _____

3. _____

4. _____

Each day, mark off the box when you successfully implement the habit.

HABIT 1	HABIT 2	HABIT 3	HABIT 4
MON ☐	MON ☐	MON ☐	MON ☐
TUE ☐	TUE ☐	TUE ☐	TUE ☐
WED ☐	WED ☐	WED ☐	WED ☐
THU ☐	THU ☐	THU ☐	THU ☐
FRI ☐	FRI ☐	FRI ☐	FRI ☐
SAT ☐	SAT ☐	SAT ☐	SAT ☐
SUN ☐	SUN ☐	SUN ☐	SUN ☐

"The things that we are obliged to do, such as hear Mass on Sunday, fast and abstain on the days appointed, etc., can become mechanical and merely habit. But it is better to be held to the Church by habit than not to be held at all. The Church is mighty realistic about human nature."

—Flannery O'Connor, letter to T. R. Spivey, August 19, 1959, quoted in _The Habit of Being_

Do you think it's better to be held to an action by habit, than not to be held at all? For instance, a habit such as kissing your spouse every night, or greeting coworkers every morning. Is it more important for such actions to be spontaneous—or to make sure they're done consistently?

_____

_____

_____

_____

_____

_____

_____

_____

_____

_____

HABITS TRACKER ✳ List the habits you're working on this week.

1. _____

2. _____

3. _____

4. _____

Each day, mark off the box when you successfully implement the habit.

HABIT 1	HABIT 2	HABIT 3	HABIT 4
MON ☐	MON ☐	MON ☐	MON ☐
TUE ☐	TUE ☐	TUE ☐	TUE ☐
WED ☐	WED ☐	WED ☐	WED ☐
THU ☐	THU ☐	THU ☐	THU ☐
FRI ☐	FRI ☐	FRI ☐	FRI ☐
SAT ☐	SAT ☐	SAT ☐	SAT ☐
SUN ☐	SUN ☐	SUN ☐	SUN ☐

Because of "tomorrow logic," we tend to feel confident that we'll be productive and virtuous—tomorrow. (The word "procrastinate" comes from *cras*, the Latin word for "tomorrow.") We're going to keep our good habits, starting tomorrow. But as Little Orphan Annie famously observed, tomorrow is always a day away.

Where do you most apply "tomorrow logic," and how can you change it?

_____

_____

_____

_____

_____

_____

_____

_____

_____

_____

_____

_____

_____

_____

*

HABITS TRACKER ✳ List the habits you're working on this week.

1. _____

2. _____

3. _____

4. _____

Each day, mark off the box when you successfully implement the habit.

HABIT 1	HABIT 2	HABIT 3	HABIT 4
MON ☐	MON ☐	MON ☐	MON ☐
TUE ☐	TUE ☐	TUE ☐	TUE ☐
WED ☐	WED ☐	WED ☐	WED ☐
THU ☐	THU ☐	THU ☐	THU ☐
FRI ☐	FRI ☐	FRI ☐	FRI ☐
SAT ☐	SAT ☐	SAT ☐	SAT ☐
SUN ☐	SUN ☐	SUN ☐	SUN ☐

To shape our habits successfully, we must know ourselves. We can't presume that if a habit-formation strategy works for one person, it will work just as well for someone else. The exercises in this book have been designed to help you better understand your habits, but also what habit-formation strategies work best for who you are.

Consider all the experiences you recorded within the pages of this journal. Leaf through your writing and browse the information in the introductory pages. Use this space to write your own "Habits Manifesto." What actions do you need to take in the future? What actions do you need to take everyday? How do you respond to habits and strategies to change habits? What are the biggest behavioral strengths and how can you use them to affect the changes you want? By setting aside this time to work on your healthy habits, you can make your life happier, healthier, and more productive.

RESOURCES *to* REQUEST

I hope that the *Better Than Before Journal* has given you many ideas about your own habits. For more, you may want to investigate my website, www.gretchenrubin.com, where I regularly post about my adventures in habit formation as well as provide suggestions and further research on habits and happiness.

I've created many additional resources on the subject of habits. You can request the following items by emailing me at gretchenrubin1@gretchenrubin.com or by downloading them through my blog:

- A copy of the template for my daily time log, as mentioned in the chapter on the Strategy of Monitoring

- A copy of my Habits Manifesto

- A copy of my Starter Kit for launching a Better Than Before habits group, as discussed in the chapter about the Strategy of Accountability; accountability groups help people swap ideas, build enthusiasm, and most important, hold each other accountable

- One-page discussion guides for book groups, for teams and work groups, and for spirituality book groups and faith-based groups

You can also email me at gretchenrubin1@gretchenrubin.com or sign up on my blog to get these free daily or monthly newletters:

- My monthly newsletter, which includes highlights from the daily blog and the Facebook page

- The daily Moment of Happiness email, which provides a great quotation on habits or happiness

- My monthly Book Club newsletter, where I recommend three books (one book about habits or happiness, one work of children's literature, and one eccentric pick)

If you'd like to volunteer as a Super-Fan, email me at gretchenrubin1@gretchenrubin.com. From time to time, I'll ask for your help (nothing too onerous, I promise) or offer a little bonus.

I also have a weekly 25-minute podcast, Happier with Gretchen Rubin, with my sister Elizabeth Craft. We talk about strategies for gaining more happiness and better habits. We're sisters, so we don't let each other get away with much!

I've written extensively about happiness, and you can also request many resources related to happiness, such as my Resolutions Chart, a Starter Kit for launching a happiness project group, discussion guides for *The Happiness Project* and *Happier at Home* for book groups and spirituality and faith-based groups, Paradoxes of Happiness, some Top Tips lists, my comic "Gretchen Rubin and the Quest for a Passion," and a copy of my Patron Saints. Email me at gretchenrubin1@gretchenrubin.com or download these resources from my blog.

For more discussion about habits and happiness, you can join the conversation on . . .

TWITTER: @gretchenrubin

LINKEDIN: GretchenRubin

FACEBOOK: GretchenRubin

YOUTUBE: GretchenRubinNY

INSTAGRAM: GretchenRubin

PINTEREST: GretchenRubin

PODCAST: Happier with Gretchen Rubin

If you'd like to email me about your own experience and views, you can reach me through my blog, www.gretchenrubin.com. All email does come straight to me. I look forward to hearing from you about this endlessly fascinating subject: the practice of everyday life.

–Gretchen Rubin